IF THE PO

"Based on firsthand experience and a personal awakening, Gret gives us the gift of story, *inviting us into a deeper understanding of global poverty and a more courageous response."*

—**PETER GREER,** PRESIDENT & CEO OF HOPE INTERNATIONAL

"He may be sometimes brash and sometimes discomforting but he is always working out of an inspired mission to stretch our minds, hearts, and souls toward the poor."

—**FRED SMITH,** FOUNDER OF THE GATHERING

"Here is a story of privilege, grace, and service—a wake-up call to live life with greater intention and generosity. Do not read this if you aren't willing to have your comfort zones challenged. It just might change the way you see everything."

—**JEFF GOINS,** BESTSELLING AUTHOR OF THE ART OF WORK

THIS BOOK WAS MADE POSSIBLE BY

PLATINUM BACKER

Alan and Beth Lee

GOLD BACKER

When The Saints

SILVER BACKERS

Robert & Elissa McNally by the grace of God

San Nicolas Assisted Living Home NW, Inc.

BACKERS

Jonathan McHugh • Andy and Lyn Campbell • The Center for Entrepreneurship + Innovation at Grove City College • Bill and Michele Moss • Andy Kangelaris • David and Cyndi Vanderpoel • Kim McKnight • Grid and Silvia Glyer • Mona Ni • Asiya Bintraafi • Ian and Katie Campbell • Paul and Cathy Addis • The Mills Family • Kenny and Lanita Cheung • Andrew Kieser • Gayle Chiasson • Bruce and Betsy Blakely • Chadwyck • George M Autry IV • Brian and Sarah Miller • Barbara Ryan • Brian and Scharlie Carlisle • Chris and Melanie Metzbower • Cody Frohmader • Kyle and Andrea Winey • Trudy Gelfand • Orlando and Myrna Briganty • Joel and Jenny Nolette • Nate and Allison Hough

ISBN 978-1-0776149-1-8

COVER DESIGN Barbara Martin

INTERNAL LAYOUT Olivier Darbonville

IN PARTNERSHIP WITH

donorsee.com

IF THE POOR WERE NEXT DOOR

HOW MOVING TO THE
POOREST COUNTRY
IN THE WORLD
INSPIRED A MISSION
TO TRANSFORM CHARITY

---

by

GRET GLYER

To my parents,
for their unrelenting
support.

TABLE OF CONTENTS

PART THREE: CYNICISM

PART FOUR: HOPE

POSTSCRIPT

ACKNOWLEDGMENTS

To make this book as clear and concise as possible, I had to leave out many amazing people who played a substantial role in the story you are about to read. There are too many names to mention, so instead, I will say that I love and appreciate you all. Thank you to everyone who has journeyed alongside me. You have left a deep impression on my heart. Also, I love you, Heather.

FOREWORD

Gret Glyer has the annoying habit of asking dangerous questions. As a young man, he looked at the changing economic landscape in the world and asked himself, "What responsibility do I have to those who are struggling just to survive?"

The answer changed everything about the way he lived. He traveled to Malawi and taught in a school. But the questions just continued. "What about the girls who don't have access to school - don't they deserve an education?"

Answering that question took Gret to places that have continued to reverberate in his life and in the lives of thousands. In "If the Poor Were Next Door," Gret tells the story of coming to grips with his moral obligation as one gifted with abundance to those on the knife's edge of survival. If God gives us good gifts, shouldn't we be passing the favor on to others?

Over the last five years, I've enjoyed discussing the implications of his response to that question with Gret. I've enjoyed partnering with him in trying to bring hope to a corner of the world. It's been fun to see him take DonorSee from a little *What if?* idea to something that is impacting the face of philanthropy.

I hope you enjoy getting to know Gret through this book, but do so at your own risk. He may ask a question that ultimately changes your life forever.

-SETH BARNES,

AUTHOR AND FOUNDER, THE WORLD RACE

PREFACE

If someone is used to flying first class, they will be upset if they are downgraded to a middle seat in coach. But if they have never flown before, they may find any spot on a plane to be an enormous life accomplishment. Two different people with two different perspectives might have opposite reactions to the same situation.

Perspective for any given situation is determined by expectations. Whatever someone is accustomed to is what they think they deserve. If their expectations are met, they are satisfied. And if they are not met, they are disappointed.

Today you are starting a book about a journey I went on that would dramatically change my perspective. I woke up one day with a particular set of expectations. And then I woke up the next day questioning every single one of those expectations.

It wasn't easy to let go of my preconceived notions and learn to embrace new ones. But it's been the most gratifying and fulfilling experience of my life.

I wrote this book so that you may benefit from what I've learned. I hope the stories inspire and provide you with guidance along your own journey.

15 facts about global poverty are scattered throughout this book - citations on page 147

"Most men lead lives of quiet desperation."

HENRY DAVID THOREAU

PART ONE

IGNORANCE

Childhood to 2013

1

I USED TO THINK **I WAS POOR**

I was the poor kid at my private school.

I had to buy used lacrosse gear instead of getting brand new equipment like my teammates, and I was never #blessed enough to get the latest pair of jeans from Abercrombie & Fitch.

When I was old enough to drive, my parents bought me a used Dodge Stratus. I was grateful for the freedom, but I was never proud of my car. I had several friends who drove brand new SUVs, and one of them drove a Mercedes-Benz.

I didn't resent my own perceived poverty. I just knew my family wasn't as wealthy as the kids who drove more expensive cars.

I later learned that attending private school and having my own car as a teenager was an enormous luxury. A luxury that few Americans get to enjoy, let alone the rest of the world.

As a private school kid, however, I was unable to appreciate how my lifestyle differed from other kids around the planet. Like most people, I just compared myself to those with whom I lived daily life.

I call this the "fish tank principle." Imagine an angelfish who lives with other angelfish. Their tank water is kept crystal clear, and they are fed delicious fish food twice a day. If these are the waters they have swum in all their lives, then it's understandable if they think all fish get to enjoy the same environmental conditions.

One day, someone might try to explain to the angelfish that other fish around the world live in algae-infested tanks and are continually fighting off common but preventable diseases. It would be difficult for a well-kept angelfish to understand these living conditions on an intellectual level. They would find it challenging to grasp how it must feel to live in algae for months and years at a time. They couldn't possibly understand the difficulty of this life on an emotional level. That experience would be too foreign for a fish who has only ever known crystal clear water.

That was me as a private school kid. My surroundings, both at school and in my neighborhood, were full of other families who were like me. I thought my life was below average because I didn't drive a fancy car. If someone tried to tell me that there are kids in the world who don't have enough food to eat, I don't think I would have found it that alarming. I had no frame of reference to understand what starvation really looks like. That lifestyle was too drastically different than mine.

I'm sure if I had lived next door to some of these poor people from the other side of the world, I might have started wondering why our lives were so different. But my fish tank didn't have people like that in it. It was just comprised of other private school kids who drove luxury cars and wore fancy jeans. It was all I knew.

21% of births globally happen without the assistance of a skilled attendant

2

1000x **RICHER**

When I was in ninth grade, my parents surprised my sister and me with a trip to Kenya. Not to go on a short-term mission trip, but to do a full-on, two-week safari in the Serengeti. We saw lions, hippos, cheetahs, rhinos, hyenas and basically every other animal featured in *The Lion King*.

This was very different than a trip to the zoo. These animals were in the wild: hunting, eating, hiding, and running. They were so used to the open-top Jeeps that a lion once used our vehicle for cover while it crept up on an unsuspecting antelope. It was so close I could have stuck my arm out the window to pet it.

Seeing these incredible beasts in the wild, however, was

not the most memorable part of the trip for me. The most significant part came after our plane first landed in Kenya.

A taxi was scheduled to drive us from the airport to where we would be staying in Nairobi. My family and our suitcases were crammed into a rundown taxi that drove through the city with alarming boldness. I was in the back seat looking out the window.

My ninth-grade eyes were seeing, for the first time, extreme poverty. I saw people living in shacks on the side of the road, and not just a few of them. They lined the streets the entire drive from the airport to the resort where we would be staying. Miles and miles of men, women, and children who had nothing but a metallic shack with a dirt floor. They wore ragged clothes and had little to no meat on their bones.

I started wondering to myself as I took in the sea of souls we were whizzing by... *Is this where they live all the time? Did they grow up here? Where do these young kids go to school?*

For all I remember, that drive may have taken five minutes or a full hour. When we arrived at the resort, I'll never forget what happened next.

Our taxi pulled up to two massive doors. They opened, and we drove inside. The drive from the entrance to the welcome center was different. Instead of the streets being lined with poverty, they were now lined with beautiful tropical trees.

We got out of the car. Some men came to get our luggage, and a butler presented us with a silver tray of warm, moist towels. We picked them up and rubbed them on our faces. I blinked as I looked around at the perfectly landscaped resort. Many thoughts raced through my head, but my mind fixated on one: *I wonder what the people outside these walls think about us?*

As we sat in the welcome center, waiting for our room, I started asking my mom and dad questions.

I have a numbers-oriented mind. I use numbers to make sense of the world. With a few carefully placed questions, I deduced that this vacation was costing our family about $1,000/day. I had also heard that there were people on the planet who survived on $1/day.

I assumed that if anyone was living on $1/day, then it had to be the people we just drove by outside. So, after a few calculations, I proudly went up to my parents with my findings.

3

UNCOMFORTABLE REALITIES

My parents were understandably not thrilled to be presented with these numbers. This vacation was something for which they had saved up for a long time. They are both hard-working people, and they were proud to have organized this trip for our family.

At the time, I didn't understand why my parents were reluctant to talk about the numbers. All I was doing was presenting facts. These facts pointed to a reality about the wealth disparity between my family and those outside the resort. I just thought it was a stimulating conversation to bring up.

The more I pressed my parents on the numbers, the less they wanted to hear it. They became irritable, so I decided to drop the conversation altogether.

The rest of our vacation was incredible. At one point, we took a hot air balloon over the Serengeti and watched lions hunt gazelle from a bird's eye view. When we went home, it didn't take long for my high school mind to forget all about the people outside the resort. I was too busy dealing with puberty and playing Halo.

Even though I had been momentary neighbors with the global poor, going back to my developed world fish tank made it easy to forget what I saw.

Global poverty was a topic of conversation that was easy to avoid. It was rarely, if ever, mentioned in my private school circles. Anyone who broached the subject would be bringing up an odd topic that made the group feel awkward.

Most people, myself included, are not eager to willingly subject themselves to uncomfortable realities. Especially as a teenager, it's easier to focus on the things that provide immediate satisfaction.

Like a moth drawn to a flame, I was drawn to whatever was fun or exciting. This usually just meant eating Chipotle or goofing off with my friends. Taking responsibility and thinking about others requires thoughtful, hard work. I wasn't naturally going to focus on uncomfortable ideas when there were so many ways to spend my time that provided instant gratification.

For the most part, my life stayed easy all the way through both high school and college. It wasn't until I graduated that my comfort became uncomfortable.

4

PRAYING THAT GOD EXISTS

I graduated from college in 2012 with a business degree. Before graduation, I had landed a job with a reputable corporation that had 16,000 employees.

Initially, I found my new job exciting. I was living on my own for the first time, and I was thriving in this competitive, cutthroat environment. I was promoted after six months, setting a record for the fastest promotion in company history. An upper-level executive pulled me aside and told me he was impressed, and that if I stuck with the company, it wouldn't be long before I had a fat paycheck, a cushy job, and a company car: they were going to fast-track me.

Despite all the fantastic incentives, this was the most depressing time of my entire life. The company was holding out carrots that I was not interested in chasing.

I didn't want to spend 20-plus years of my life in a corporate environment. I was totally replaceable. If I quit, they would just give my spot to the next hotshot gunning for my position. To the company and the customers we served, my personal contribution was negligible. I didn't want to wake up in 20 years and regret spending most of my waking hours serving a large corporation in exchange for a cushy lifestyle. To me, that future was like looking into the abyss.

I didn't know much, but I knew I didn't want to be working there anymore, pouring hours into something I honestly didn't believe in. Still, I had no idea where I should go next or what to do with my life. No clue. Zero direction.

This caused me to start asking the most foundational questions a person can possibly ask. I had been a Christian since high school, but I found myself doubting whether there really was a loving God who actually had a plan for my life.

I came to the conclusion that there are two possibilities: either God exists, which meant there was potential for my life to have meaning, or there is no God, and therefore, everything was meaningless. The way I saw things, at the end of the day, there is no meaning to be found for a random clump of cells on a rock hurtling through space. There would be an ocean of time before me and an ocean of time after me. Anything I did on this unspecial rock would be of no permanent consequence. Unless, of course, there was an infinite Being outside of time and space that created me for a meaningful purpose.

At night I would get on my knees and say, “God, I pray that you exist,” over and over again. I knew the prayer made no sense, but I didn’t know what else to do. The stakes could not have been higher. If God existed, there was hope that I may someday find a meaningful calling for my life. If not, nothing I ever do or say would matter. I badly wanted God to exist, but I also wanted to live in reality. If there was no God, that was something I was going to have to accept.

5

STATIC

My stint of existential angst lasted for months. My prayers, crying out for God to exist, were a nightly activity. It was during this time that I attended a weekly evening prayer meeting at my church. I didn't let them know what I was going through, because I was seen as a leader in this setting. Despite being a leader on the outside, internally, I struggled with dread and anxiety.

These meetings would include prayer and then a family-style dinner. After we dismissed for the evening, I would drive home by myself.

In the summer, I always drove with the windows down and the music blaring. One evening, for a reason I can't remember, I drove home in silence with the windows up. My favorite part of the drive was a long country road with green farmland on either side and a windmill off in the distance.

As I approached the windmill, the trip odometer on my car's dashboard read "94.1." I figured it must have been the last time I reset it. I thought about it for a moment and then moved on. I looked down again thinking plenty of time had passed but noticed that the reading hadn't changed. I began fixating on that number.

I can't explain it now, but something told me to turn on my radio and tune to station 94.1. I turned the knob until my dashboard matched the trip odometer, but I heard nothing except for static.

"Well, so much for that," I thought. I reached to turn off the radio, but something told me to keep listening.

It was a strange inclination, but I had nothing to lose. I pulled my hand away from the knob and continued listening to nothing for another 30 seconds. The static remained constant as I got closer and closer to the windmill.

Then, right as I passed the windmill—my absolute favorite part of the drive—a song came through the radio. Just one lyric that was unmistakably clear, as if it had been beamed specifically into my car.

Clear as day, I heard a line from a popular hit song: *"Don't you worry, don't you worry child. See heaven's got a plan for you."*

Just as quickly as the music appeared, it cut out, and the static returned. I slammed the knob of the radio to turn it off and started weeping. God had spoken to me.

6

REGRET MINIMIZATION FRAMEWORK

People often speculate about how involved God is in our daily lives. I don't pretend to know how that works. All I know is there are many stories, like mine, where a particular message is delivered to someone so precisely that it seems to defy coincidence.

I worked for another six months at my corporate job after the "radio incident," but things were different now.

I didn't know what was coming or what was in store, but somehow, I was profoundly at peace. I truly believed that I would someday discover a meaningful calling for my life. Even during the monotony of a dry office job, I was able to trust and hope that purpose would come from it all.

On June 30, 2013, I was a groomsman in a wedding. One of my best friends was getting married in Charlottesville,

Virginia. I overheard one of the other groomsmen talking about his upcoming job after the summer. He was going to be a teacher in Malawi, Africa. His name was Woody.

"So, what are you doing in Malawi?" I asked him.

"I'm going to be a history teacher. I'm pretty nervous about it," he replied.

"Don't be nervous, man. I'll be working a boring corporate job for the next year of my life, and you'll be teaching kids in Africa. I'm almost jealous of you."

"Well, I think they still have a vacant position."

"Ha, sounds fun. But I definitely don't know anything about teaching. I guess I could maybe teach math, but even that sounds far-fetched."

"I think the spot they have left to fill is for a math teacher."

Numbers always made sense to me. The opportunity to escape my corporate job had just unexpectedly fallen into my lap.

After the wedding, the next time I would see Woody was precisely 30 days later at the airport, with a one-way ticket to Malawi. In that time, I had quit my job, received my shots, and re-taught myself Algebra 2 and Pre-Calculus. It was a quick transition that puzzled many of the people at my work. My boss even offered me a raise to get me to stay, but my mind was made up.

Jeff Bezos, CEO of Amazon, coined the term *Regret Minimization Framework*, which helped me make my decision. The idea was that it's easiest to make pivotal life decisions when you ask yourself, "Which choice will I regret the least when I'm 80 years old?" I knew of countless people who had expressed regret over not traveling more when they were young. That made the idea of moving to Malawi a little easier to accept.

Some of my close friends also tried to talk me out of going. They knew I was in search of spiritual growth, and they insisted I could find it by staying in America. I agreed that it was a possibility in the same way it's possible to get in peak physical condition by working out in a cake shop. The reality is, however, it's easier to get in shape by signing up for CrossFit. I had a hunch that my personal development would be fast-tracked by moving to Africa.

That said, I wasn't thinking so clearly at the time. It was a mad rush as I had 30 days to prepare for my year abroad. I had no idea what I was getting myself into, I just knew almost anything would be better than my suffocating corporate job.

As Woody and I were boarding the airplane, I leaned over to him and said, "It's so weird that I took my last hot shower for a year this morning."

"You think so?" Woody replied back.

In my ignorance, I somehow believed I would be living in a grass-thatched hut for the next year of my life. I didn't know how wrong I would be. Upon arrival, we were driven to the compound that would be our new home. We had not only hot water, but also electricity, internet, a gym, and a wonderful community. Malawi, at first glance, was not what I had expected.

And yet, just outside our compound walls were people who had similar lifestyles to those I saw during my family vacation in Kenya. I was most definitely not in the comfort of my "fish tank" anymore.

"You may choose to look the other way but you can never say again that you did not know."

WILLIAM WILBERFORCE

PART TWO

AWARENESS

2013

7

WHAT'S MINE IS **YOURS**

I had countless adventures during my first few months in Malawi. One time, I went sailing with friends, and our boat capsized. As we were rescued, a hippo surfaced right where we had fallen into the water. It had been swimming right below us.

Another time, my roommates and I had to kill two spitting cobras in our front yard. These cobras shoot venom right into people's eyes and blind them. We timidly used machetes to get the job done.

Maybe the most exciting adventure was when I was charged with resisting arrest my second week after arrival. The policemen let me off with an inexpensive fine, and we later became friends.

But one story from those first few months left a more profound impression on me than all those others combined.

Every Friday, I would visit a nearby village where a Malawian man named Blessings held an afternoon program for the local kids. The kids liked it when Americans attended this weekly event. They got a kick out of our light skin and how bad we were at soccer.

The structure of the afternoon was simple. The children sang worship songs, were read a Bible lesson, discussed the lesson in a small group, and were finally given play time. I would watch from the back as the local Malawians ran the whole event.

The leaders would occasionally ask me to help out during the small group session. In one such instance, I was instructed to monitor ten Malawian boys as they colored. I took the group of five-year-olds to a log that served as a make-shift bench. The boys sat on the log, with hot sand under their bare feet and a sparsely leafed tree that served as shade. Grass-thatched village huts were scattered around us.

As I pulled out the coloring materials, what happened next can best be described as a veil being lifted from my eyes.

I only had five coloring sheets and five crayons for all ten of the boys. When I handed them over, the boys grabbed the materials and immediately got to work.

They occasionally would say something to each other in Chichewa, their native language, but for the most part, they just wanted to color.

They weren't bothered by the lack of materials for a second. Five boys took a single coloring sheet, and the other five took a single crayon. One boy would hold the paper while the other would color with his one crayon. When a boy wanted a different color, he would ask to trade. Sometimes the boys with the sheets wanted a turn to color, so they swapped.

As the ten boys swapped their five crayons around, I was reminded of my childhood. I would sit in air-conditioned classrooms with a full arsenal of crayons, markers, glue, construction paper, and more at my disposal. It was all mine and whatever I didn't use would get thrown away at the end of the year, only to be totally replaced the next year.

Something in my mind clicked into place. Up until this day, there was a distance between myself and the poor. I saw them, saw how they lived, but I never empathized with them. There was too much of a lifestyle gap for me to connect with them on an emotional level. It wasn't until I saw these boys doing a familiar activity that I realized the shocking reality.

For them, ten boys sharing five crayons was normal. They didn't know anything else. For myself, and the fish tank I swam in growing up, this wasn't normal. If one of my classmates only had access to half a crayon, I would be worried about them.

The more I observed the innocent Malawian boys as they colored, the more I comprehended that there was one thing that separated us more than anything else: where we were born.

Through no effort of my own, I was born into a loving family in a wealthy suburb outside of Washington, D.C. They were born in a remote village in rural Africa, and that one factor meant that our lives would be unfathomably different. This reality had been right in front of me ever since my trip to Kenya. It wasn't until now that I had accepted it.

8

HUNTING FOR **BAD GUYS**

During my first year in Malawi, most of my time was not spent in rural villages, like the scene described in the last chapter. Most of my time was spent on the compound where I taught high school math to missionary kids and upper-class Malawians.

The compound was large, about one square mile, and was comprised of several houses and the school where I taught. I lived in a house with five other guys my age and my roommate Woody.

One night, at about 1 a.m., Woody and I were watching a pirated TV show on my laptop before falling asleep. In the middle of an episode, we heard whistles blowing outside. I looked out the barred window and saw guards running up and down the compound.

I picked up a hiking stick for protection and walked outside. There were some large bushes in our front yard that were rustling.

I began to get nervous because I had heard stories of people being robbed on our compound before. It was usually done with machetes, which would outmatch the hiking stick I was wielding.

Two grown men came out of the bushes, and my heart skipped a beat. I swallowed. Then I felt a sigh of relief. The two men were our guards.

"What's going on?" I asked.

"There are intruders on campus," they replied back with a thick accent.

"Do you guys need help?" I said, expecting them to say no.

"Yes."

I gulped. I went back inside my house and told Woody what was going on. We both followed the guards, each nervously clutching our own hiking sticks with both hands.

Soon we joined up with the rest of the men on campus. Some were wielding weapons, and some were not.

The report was that two men were spotted. They had climbed over our compound walls and shimmied down a water tower. We lost track of them, but one thing was known for sure: the intruders were still within our walls.

I could have hidden in my house and not joined the search party, but that would mean fewer people to sweep the compound and find the two intruders. It would also mean less safety for whoever made first contact.

We broke up into pairs and began looking around. We threw items into trees and checked every dark corner of the compound. After two full hours of searching, we found nothing.

This incident helped me appreciate the lesson that the ten Malawian boys had taught me. It's a lesson that I had to live personally to grasp fully.

In some parts of the world, there is a true lack of resources. In those environments, everyone has to pitch in. Everyone has to bear some responsibility for what happens to the group. Otherwise, the entire community will suffer. When there are scarce resources, selfishness stands out like a sore thumb.

The next morning the news broke that the "two intruders" were actually my friends Bill and Dani. They had been on a secret date on top of the water tower. They didn't want anyone to know they had been seeing each other. Unfortunately for them, their plan backfired.

9

THE FLIP

I loved going to the village on Friday afternoons. It was like a reset every week. No matter what was going on in my life, going to that village was a great way to reorient my perspective. It made me realize that all my problems were so insignificant. I would leave every week feeling refreshed and rejuvenated.

There was one exception.

Once, while out in the village, I received a phone call that there had been an accident. People I knew were involved, and it didn't look good.

I ran over to Blessings, the coordinator of the Friday event and he agreed to drive me the 30 minutes back to the compound.

I hopped into the passenger seat of his white truck, and we sped off. On the drive, I tried calling people I knew, but the reception was spotty, and the lines were busy. I was only able to talk to people for about twenty seconds at a time before the line cut out. Bit by bit, I began to piece together what had happened.

My two friends, from the water tower incident, had organized a trip to take kids from a local orphanage to Lake Malawi. A passenger van carrying Bill, Dani and thirteen orphans was driving faster than it should have been when one of the tires blew out.

The van flipped over five times, the glass of every window shattered, and many of the passengers had been flung from the vehicle. According to the intermittent phone calls, Bill and the orphans were mostly doing okay. Dani, who was now dating Bill, was not. She had gone through the windshield.

Blessings' white truck pulled up to the compound clinic, and I hopped out before it stopped moving. A crowd of Malawians had congregated outside the clinic doors. I pushed through them to get inside.

The next moments were a blur. Several people I knew were lining the hallways of the clinic, including Woody. Everyone's face had a sullen look on it, and no one was saying anything.

As I ventured deeper into the hallway, I found Bill sitting in a patient room. He was conscious but slumped over. Blood had coagulated on the tip of his nose. I tried talking to him, but the only thing he could say was, "Dani's in bad shape." He kept repeating those words over and over.

I walked across the hallway, just outside the operating room. The door flung open, and I saw Dani lying on the operating table. A blonde woman named Amy was holding her head in place. Amy saw me standing outside and yelled, "Gret! Get in here! We need you!"

10

DEATH SENTENCE

During the water tower incident, all the men pitched in to keep the campus safe. Had even one man stayed behind, it would have made everyone feel less secure. When Dani's van flipped over, I now realized that pitching in was more than a matter of security. In this case, it was a matter of life and death.

I walked through the operating room doors and approached Dani's limp body lying on the table. Amy asked me to hold Dani's legs down. She was unconscious, but her lower body was fidgeting. Keeping her legs in place was meant to prevent further injury, which could result in paralysis.

As I stood there, holding her legs down, I looked at Dani. She had a neck brace on and was turning gray.

I then looked around. The other victims of the accident were scattered across the room. Some were crying out in agony. Others laid in silent shock. I had never felt so much chaos around me at once.

A nurse walked by, and Amy alerted her that Dani was turning gray. They took her oxygen levels and found that they were depleting fast. And there was nothing they could do. She needed to be rushed to the Intensive Care Unit at the city hospital.

Dani was loaded into an ambulance and taken to Lilongwe Hospital. Amy and I followed closely behind.

By the time we'd arrived and parked, Dani had been taken into a back room for some tests. Amy went with her, and I stayed in the hallway.

After a few minutes, Amy came out. She was crying. She looked me right in the eyes and with a shaky voice, said, "Okay, we really need to pray. The doctors found bleeding in Dani's brain, and they're saying she'll be dead by 8 p.m. tonight."

Some doctors rushed in between us and broke up our conversation. I walked down the hospital hallway in a daze, found a stoop outside, and sat down. I repeated, over and over, the only words I could think of: "God, please heal Dani."

Ten minutes later, I walked back into the hospital hallway.

What I'm about to tell you can be interpreted in two different ways. One way is to look at it from a purely rational perspective and assume nothing supernatural happened. The other way is to leave open the possibility that supernatural events might happen, even if we can retroactively conjure up a loosely rational explanation for them.

I found Amy back in the hallway, still in tears but different tears this time. She told me that the doctors misread Dani's brain scan. When they went back to look, there was no internal bleeding. Dani's survival chances had just skyrocketed.

From my perspective, I had just received a direct answer to prayer. I don't know how God orchestrated the events. But I believe it's possible that there was bleeding in Dani's brain until I prayed, and then God reversed it. Others may dismiss these events as mere coincidence. I'm not saying that's impossible. I just find it more probable that a loving God deliberately orchestrated a miracle. From my perspective, and based on many other experiences in my life, that was the best explanation.

Dani had to be medevaced via airplane down to a hospital in South Africa. She was in a coma for three weeks, but she survived.

I later learned that right after the van flipped over, two ambulances showed up. They "just happened" to be driving by. There's no "9-1-1" in Malawi. The appearance of two ambulances on the scene, in the poorest country on the planet, minutes after the crash, was another miracle.

A year after her accident, Dani returned to Malawi to teach another full year. She also ran a half marathon, despite having to heal from five broken bones in her back and neck. Her story was one miracle after another. A few years after that, she also married Bill.

But right after her accident, there was still one thing that bothered both her and me.

Although the thirteen orphans survived, they would have died if they had sustained the same injuries as Dani. They didn't have health insurance and wouldn't have gotten an emergency plane ride to South Africa. It would have been over for them. Dani, on the other hand, survived because she was from a wealthy suburban family from Colorado who could afford a high-end insurance package. She didn't earn that, it was just the situation she was born into. That meant that she would survive in a scenario where most others would die.

Dani's story was miraculous. I believe the mercy of God was on full display, but so was the unfairness of the world. I would eventually have to reckon with that.

11

THE HANDSHAKE

Blessings, the man who coordinated the Friday village trips, was himself from a remote part of Malawi. He was born eight hours from the closest hospital. His village had no access to clean water, but he somehow managed to make it to the city, go to college and eventually get his master's degree in America before returning to Malawi to continue serving his people.

The more I got to know Blessings, the more I respected him and what he had accomplished.

One day, as Blessings was driving me home from a village trip, I unwittingly told him, "If you ever need extra help with anything, just let me know."

I didn't think much of it at the time, but Blessings didn't forget. He came knocking on my front door a few days later. He wanted to show me something and asked me to hop into his white truck. We drove twenty minutes down an asphalt road and another twenty minutes down a dirt road until we pulled up to a village that I had never been to before.

I got out of the truck and was greeted by a plump chief, who gave me a big smiley handshake. Blessings exchanged a few words in Chichewa with the chief as we all started walking into the heart of the village.

We walked for several minutes. As we walked, we passed grass-thatched huts, kids playing in the dirt and women cooking over an open flame on the ground. Off in the distance, I saw a gaunt figure kneeling in an open area between a few huts. As we approached the figure, I began to see I was looking at an elderly woman. She used her staff to get onto her feet and hobbled towards us. When she was just a few feet away, she collapsed onto the ground and laid her staff aside. She stuck out her hand, and I shook it.

I looked at Blessings and asked, "Why did you bring me here?"

Blessings explained the 70-year-old widow's situation. Her name was Rosina, and she was literally skin and bones. Up until that point, I had never seen a human who was actually starving to death.

Rosina's son was an abusive alcoholic who regularly beat her. She used to live in his house but had to flee when the beatings got too severe. She now lived in a small, brick room that was about seven feet in diameter and had basketball-sized holes in her roof.

The rainy season was coming in one month, and if she didn't get a place to live, she would likely die from over-exposure to the elements.

To make things worse, Rosina hadn't eaten any food in seven days.

After learning all this, I knew why Blessings had brought me to this village. He cared about Rosina and was afraid for her life.

"A single death is a tragedy, a million deaths is a statistic."

JOSEPH STALIN

PART THREE

CYNICISM

2013 to 2014

12

FACE TO FACE

It takes a while for most people to grasp the harsh reality of extreme poverty with full clarity. That was the case with me. Anyone who grew up in the developed world has no frame of reference for just how impoverished other humans on our planet are. People think poverty in America is comparable to poverty in Sub-Saharan Africa. In some ways, that's true. People do get stuck in cycles of poverty in the developed world. For the most part, though, global poverty is exponentially worse.

I could tell you a thousand statistics about why these different types of poverty are barely worth comparing. For example, there is a direct correlation in America between poverty and obesity. In other words, the poorest Americans are also typically the most overweight Americans. By contrast, in Sub-Saharan Africa, the poorest people are starving to death. But statistics rarely persuade people, so I don't bring them up very much.

The only thing that genuinely convinces people is if they see poverty with their own eyes. It's not until they see a baby starving or a child die from dirty water that they truly grasp it. If Rosina were your next door neighbor, you would get it. You would understand how horrifying and complicated extreme poverty is. However, Rosina is tucked away in a remote village. The eyes of the world pay little attention to people like her.

I don't blame anyone for that. Creating awareness about global poverty is like swimming against the current. In fact, I had no idea that people like her existed until she was kneeling right in front of me.

It wasn't until I was face to face with her, and the uncomfortable reality of extreme poverty, that I felt compelled to act. To do something. Anything.

The first thing I did was pay about $7 to get Rosina a bag of food that would last her a month. Sadly, food wasn't her most pressing concern. She needed a place to live. Blessings told me that he brought me out to meet Rosina because he was hoping we could help build her a house.

I somehow knew he was going to ask that, and I dreaded the question. Where I'm from, houses cost about $400,000 on average.

I figured it would be less than that in the poorest country on the planet, I just didn't know how much less. I was thinking a house in Malawi would cost in the $10,000 to $20,000 range. Even if I wanted to buy her a house, I still had no clue where the money would come from. At the time, I was barely able to cover my own expenses while living off my teacher's stipend of $600 a month.

"Blessings, how much would it cost to build her a house?"

"Eight hundred dollars."

I had to ask several clarifying questions just to be sure, but it all added up. For the price of an iPad, Rosina could get a brand new house. It would even have cement floors and a tin roof, which would be considered a luxury in her village.

I had Blessings take a video of me explaining the situation. I knew my friends from back home would be eager to send money my way so Rosina could get her house. Her condition was so dire, and the price was shockingly affordable.

I uploaded my video and emailed it out to my closest friends with a PayPal link. Due to the impending rainy season, time was of the essence.

A few days went by, and there was near radio silence. Except for a single $100 donation, everyone else had ignored me, and they had ignored Rosina. I was appalled.

13

SHE WOKE UP **SCREAMING**

A year before I met Teleza, she woke her family up in the middle of the night with a blood-curdling scream. Her dad rushed into her room and found her in great agony.

She was five-years-old when she lost her hearing. We have no idea what caused it. We just know it suddenly happened that one night.

My friends and I had seen miracles happen before. So we decided to find Teleza every week and ask God to heal her of her deafness. This would become one of our traditions during our weekly Friday village trips. We would gather around her, along with several Malawian kids, and we would pray for quick and immediate healing.

I can't say whether or not I really expected God to answer my prayers, but I definitely had an open mind to it. If Teleza miraculously got her hearing back, I would not have been dumbfounded.

After many, many weeks of prayer, Teleza remained deaf. It didn't seem like our prayers were working.

I've had to learn that my timeline is irrelevant to the plans of God. I might want things to happen right now, but it doesn't always work that way.

Eventually, after several more weeks of prayer, we learned that there was an audiology clinic that might be able to fit her with some hearing aids. We spoke with the clinicians, and they said that there was a strong possibility that "bone-conduction" hearing aids could help Teleza. They would use vibrations to get discernable sounds into her brain.

With cautious optimism, we brought Teleza into the clinic to get her fitted. The clinicians took her into a soundproof booth and did some preliminary tests. She began to raise her hand up and down.

It looked like it was working. An ounce of hope crept up into me. I used to think, "It would be so much easier to believe in God if my prayers about Teleza were answered." This was about to be a pivotal moment in my life.

The clinician came out of the booth with a smile

on her face. She closed the door behind her and said the preliminary tests were looking really good. Teleza was going to get her hearing back! God had answered my prayers.

Now, allow me to take a quick break from that story to explain that deafness in America is very different than deafness in Malawi. America has a robust infrastructure in place so that hearing-impaired people can still participate in modern society. Sign language, closed captioning, and schools for the deaf all allow hearing-impaired people to thrive. In Malawi, on the other hand, deafness is an ugly fate. No one speaks sign language, and there's a high illiteracy rate. Someone who can't hear is resigned to a future of near zero communication with other human beings. This also makes deaf women a prime candidate for rape because they are unable to report their attackers. Deafness in Malawi is often a life of loneliness and abuse.

I can't explain the amount of hope and relief I felt when that clinician walked out of the sound booth. I thought back to the time, not that long ago, when I would stay up late at night saying: "God, I pray that you exist." Here was the reason for my suffering. God wanted to bring me to this moment and show me that my prayers matter. That I matter.

I was witnessing the impossible unfold before my very eyes. Whatever else happened in my life, I could always remember back to the time that God healed a girl of deafness right in front of me.

A second clinician came in to test Teleza and fit her with her new hearing aids. He went into the sound booth and performed the same test. We watched, this time with excitement and eager anticipation.

But something wasn't working. Teleza wasn't raising her hand like last time, and the clinician kept fiddling with the equipment. He had a frown on his face as he called in his colleague. They tried testing Teleza together, but nothing was working.

We soon deduced that there was an issue with the first round of tests. Whenever there was a beep for Teleza to raise her hand, a red light also went off. So Teleza was raising her hand because of the light, not because of the beep. Once it was covered up, she stopped raising her hand, and we knew with certainty that she was hearing nothing but silence. Teleza had been sentenced to a life of deafness. A life that's almost too horrible to imagine.

I stared at Teleza in disbelief. It felt like I loved her more than God did. I was the one who prayed for her every week. I was the one who brought her into the audiology clinic. I was the one who wanted her to hear again.

The God who is capable of creating an entire universe was sitting back and allowing the continuation of immense suffering. I saw no justification for this inaction. Anger and confusion festered inside of me as my whole worldview collapsed. The unfairness of the world was again standing in front of me, but this time in vivid detail.

14

THE MAN ON THE **CELL PHONE**

As a reminder, I had a day job as a teacher for my first year in Malawi. I taught Algebra 2 and Pre-Calculus to high school missionary kids and upper-class Malawians.

The kids I taught were such good kids. They were respectful, eager to learn, and valued their education immensely because they knew how lucky they were in comparison to the kids right outside the compound walls. They also took care of each other, and they grew up thousands of miles away from the materialism that saturates American culture. They just valued relationships, sports, and doing their best. I loved teaching them.

One of my students, Mzati, was a super smart kid. He would tell you with cocky confidence that he was one of my favorite students, but I told him the same thing I said to all the others: "Sorry, I dislike all my students equally."

Mzati always walked home from school, but he was supposed to get back before dark. He stayed a little later one day because he was selling soccer jerseys to some of the teachers on the compound.

As he was walking home, he saw a guy on a cell phone right in front of his parents' gated house. As he got closer, the man with the cell phone looked at him. Then Mzati felt it: a machete blade struck the top of his head. Someone had snuck up on him from behind, and the man with the cell phone joined in on the attack.

The two attackers pushed him to the ground and continued to whack him with machetes. In a burst of adrenaline, Mzati kicked one of the attackers in the chest. They grabbed his backpack and ran away.

Blood was pouring down his face and shirt. The adrenaline gave him enough stamina to walk inside. His mother was in the middle of a Bible study when her bloody son limped into the living room.

15

$20 HOSPITAL TRIP

When I went into the village on Friday's, there was a little girl in a purple dress that would cheer on the boys playing soccer. Blessings told me her name was Emily. She was seven years old and had one of the most infectious smiles I have ever seen.

Two years before I met Emily, her mother became seriously ill. When Blessings learned about it, he tried to arrange a trip to the hospital.

A hospital trip would have cost $20. However, when you live on $1/day, all your money goes toward survival. Emily's mom was unable to afford the cost, so Blessings sent an email to an American friend asking for the $20 to pay for hospital expenses. His friend, not realizing the severity of the situation, declined the request.

Six months later, this American friend visited Malawi on a short term mission trip. Blessings was leading the team on a tour through the village when they came across Emily's mom lying in agony on the ground. "What happened to her?" the group asked, in shock.

"Remember the lady who needed $20?" Blessings replied, "This is her. She was never admitted to the hospital."

The team changed all of their plans for the trip. Their new priority was to save the life of Emily's mom. They spent the next two weeks taking her to different hospitals, buying her medicine, and providing her with healthy foods.

At the end of their trip, the group boarded a plane to go home. They had done everything in their power to heal Emily's mom. When they arrived in America, they received word that, despite all their efforts, she had passed away.

Hearing Emily's story made me realize just how different other people in our world live. This beautiful, smiling girl in a purple dress was an orphan because her mother couldn't afford a $20 hospital trip.

16

THE BOY **WITH A RED BALL**

I have just told you four stories that include deep anguish in the lives of real people.

The suffering I saw in Malawi was far worse than anything I had been exposed to growing up. Not only was it hard to watch, but I worried that it meant that there was no loving God. I would never want someone I loved to suffer from poverty, rape, violence, or the many other things that humans have to endure. It didn't make sense to me that God would sit back and do nothing while countless people around the world suffered.

Then I heard a simple analogy and realized I may not have the full picture.

Think about a three-year-old boy with a red ball. The boy loses his grip on the ball, and it bounces into the street. He eagerly chases after his toy, totally unaware of the oncoming traffic. Thankfully, before he makes it to the road, his father picks him up and rescues him, but the boy doesn't like this. He screams and kicks his father and cries out, "Why, Daddy? Why!?" No amount of consolation can assure the boy. He just watched his favorite toy bounce right under a tire that crushed it. No matter what his father says, and no matter how much love his father shows, the boy is inconsolable. From his perspective, his suffering is meaningless, and his father doesn't love him.

I found this analogy easy to understand but difficult to accept. Logically, it makes sense that if an adult can have more wisdom than a child, then surely, the Creator of the universe is wiser than any human. I think the way God looks at our pain might be similar to how that father looked at his crying three-year-old. He was sad to see his child upset, but he allowed it to happen for a greater good, and someday, his boy will thank him for that.

There's no question that suffering is still painful for all of us, even if we believe that there is some grand reason behind it. When I was being exposed to the suffering of my friends in Malawi, I often thought of the story where Jesus learns that his good friend Lazarus has died. Even though he knew he was going to raise Lazarus from the dead moments later, Jesus' first reaction was to weep. He cried for his friend because of the sadness he felt at that moment.

We may someday get a satisfying answer for why our world is full of immense suffering, but that doesn't make the tragedy less real today. It still hurts. Life is hard, but I think it will someday all make sense, as impossible as that may sound.

In the meantime, it's okay to weep.

"When something is important enough, you do it even if the odds are not in your favor."

ELON MUSK

PART FOUR

HOPE

2014 to 2016

17

THE ARC

One of the beautiful things about this life is that sometimes you do get to watch the arc of redemption play out right in front of you with unmistakable clarity. You get to see the meaning behind suffering unfold in real time.

Mzati made a full recovery from his machete attack. His attackers were found and put in prison. One afternoon, after school, I drove Mzati out to the prison. He shared his story to 300 inmates. He said, "I believe if I had died that night, I would have gone to hell. I was not living a good life at the time. I'm glad the attack happened because it was a wake-up call for me." Mzati then paused and looked at his audience. He knew his attackers were watching. He then spoke some very brave words for a fifteen-year-old: "And to the men who attacked me that night, I forgive you."

Months after Teleza's appointment, I was sitting around a dinner table with some visitors from England. They had come to serve at the audiology clinic where Teleza's fate was pronounced. I overheard them talking about a surgeon who would be flying in. They had a big problem, but I had a solution.

Thanks to a large donation, a surgeon from the U.K. would be visiting to perform the first-ever cochlear implant surgery on two children in Malawi. This was a $50,000 procedure where a chip would be implanted inside the child's head, giving hearing to someone who was totally deaf. It can only be done on kids of a certain age, and it only works if the child learned to speak before they became deaf. The only problem was that one of the kids they were supposed to operate on had disappeared. He had stopped showing up for his preliminary appointments. The audiologists needed a specific type of child with deafness, and they needed one fast.

We again brought Teleza in to see if she fit the criteria for this surgery. She did, she got the surgery, and she now has her hearing back.

I love Teleza's story because it's the perfect example of something working out better than if I had gotten exactly what I wanted. Had God answered my prayer immediately, I would have been tempted to perceive that God's primary function was that of a genie, granting whatever wishes I prayed hard enough for. And what a shallow and one-dimensional view of God that would have been. Instead, not only did the miracle of Teleza hearing again affirm my belief in God, but I also learned a vital lesson in trust.

When I asked my friends for help to build Rosina a house, and they didn't donate, I was devastated. It seemed like such an excellent opportunity to make a lasting difference in the life of a widow.

My immediate reaction was cynicism. I started thinking about how materialistic Americans are, and how they spend money on frivolous things but won't pony up a little cash for a dying widow. I'm not going to lie: I was judgmental. But I was also depressed. It broke my heart that they would so easily dismiss Rosina.

After about a week, I collected myself. Rosina still needed a house, and I still needed to find the remaining $700. Her life was on the line. Every second I spent wallowing in disdain and self-pity wasn't going to change that.

I tried to gather information and figure out what was going on and learned two things.

First, I learned about donor fatigue. It wasn't that my

The average income of someone in extreme poverty is **87** cents per day friends didn't care about Rosina. It's that people with money are frequently being asked for help from those who need money. My short video didn't provide my friends with enough context for how an $800 house would help a starving widow.

The second thing I learned was that wealthy people like having spreadsheets, facts, and projections.

I put together a lengthy blog post with pie charts showing how the $800 would be spent, what the timetable was, and how the donations would make an impact that would go beyond the brick and mortar result.

Within 24 hours of emailing out the blog post, the remainder of the money came in. I got it to Blessings, and he hired everyone necessary to build Rosina her new house. A day before the most substantial downpour I had ever seen, the roof went on, and she moved in.

Rosina was spared. She had food, shelter, and people who cared about her. I thought to myself, "If this is the only thing I ever do for Malawi, I'm proud of it."

18

THE 60/40 DECISION

After the success of Rosina's house, I built up a smidgen of credibility. People noticed that I was responsible with the funds they donated, and this meant that more donors would be willing to trust me.

The thing was, I had no intention of going beyond building that first house. In fact, I was dead set on leaving Malawi after my first year. My roommate, and new best friend, Woody, wasn't coming back. He already had a job lined up for when he returned to the States.

Malawi was supposed to be my one year of adventure.

Before I left America, I had made a promise to myself that I would get back on a traditional career path after one year. It was the sensible thing to do.

An email from my mom caused me to rethink my plans. She was part of a painting class with other women her age. Once a week, they met at a studio to paint, drink, and chat. She had spent all year telling her painting friends about my adventures in Malawi. They fell in love with Rosina's story. My mom's email explained that they wanted to raise another $800 to build a house for a widow.

After a few weeks, the money came in, and another house was built. This time I made a video of the whole process. I used a point and shoot camera to show my mom's friends how their $800 donation was turned into a home. They were ecstatic.

Every few weeks, I would get another email from my mom. "Guess what? We raised *another* $800!"

People wanted to build houses for widows, and they loved the videos I was making to thank them.

This gave me a reason to stay in Malawi a second year and nurture what was happening, but I was still hesitant. I had a lot of good friends in America, and I felt an obligation to get back on a traditional career path.

Then, a mentor pulled me aside and told me about the concept of a *60/40 decision.* He said, "Gret, sometimes in life, you will have two great options in front of you. No matter which you pick, you will experience grief either way. Eventually, you'll have to choose the slightly better option and accept that you'll be missing out on the other path." This concept gave me peace about missing out on another year of life in America.

I resolved to stay in Malawi a second year and work full-time on building houses for orphans and widows. I set up a 501c3 and called the charity HOWMs (pronounced *homes*), which was short for "Housing for Orphans and Widows in Malawi."

I took a trip back to the States over the summer and received a gift from one of my mom's painting friends, that would again change the course of my life. She bought me a brand new DSLR camera with extra gear and lenses. In other words, a woman who had never met me before came over to my house and handed me a $2,000 present. She wanted to encourage me, and she believed in what I was doing.

And, for the first time in my life, I believed in what I was doing.

19

THE GLOBAL 1%

To date, HOWMs has constructed more than 150 houses for orphans and widows all over Malawi. We continue to build a few houses every month. Anyone who donates gets a video of the recipient moving into their new place.

There was a time when I wondered if we would ever run out of houses to build. Rosina's story was so tragic that I assumed it was rare. I was wrong.

I hear a lot of Americans angry at "The 1%." And, fair enough, but they often don't realize that they, themselves, are in the global 1%. Those who earn $34,000-a-year are wealthier than 99% of the people on this planet. What's shocking is that those who earn $1,000-a-year are wealthier than 50% of the planet, even after adjusting for cost of living. In other words, three billion people are barely scraping by on less than $3-a-day. There are far more people like Rosina roaming around our planet than most of us realize. The global population looks a lot more like her than it does like the private school fish tank in which I grew up.

Although this meant that HOWMs had plenty of room to grow, it was never meant to scale. I felt convicted to keep it small to ensure houses were being donated responsibly.

Finding a way to help people on a large scale was still an ambition of mine, I just needed a way to do that sustainably.

After some brainstorming, I came up with, "Village Fridays." It was a simple concept for a YouTube series that tied into my weekly trips to the village. Now, I would just take my camera and film someone who needed some kind of relief. Sometimes it was a baby who needed formula milk. Other times it was a woman with leprosy who needed a new roof.

The video was always in two parts. The first part was showing the result of the donations from the previous week. The second part was showing a new need to which viewers could donate.

It was a hit. People loved giving and seeing their names

in the videos after they donated. Village Fridays started off with small needs that cost $35 or $50. But soon the demand grew, and we started doing $300-plus size projects every week.

One Friday, I decided to take a significant risk. There were six weeks left before the end of 2015. So I made a video asking for $9,000 by the end of the year. I wanted to put a mosquito net in the house of every single person in the village. When 70% of the community sleeps under a mosquito net, the malaria rate in that village typically drops by 90%. Many lives would be saved.

About $1,000 came in the first week, and then the campaign stalled.

I got an email from an old friend from college saying that he wanted to dedicate his birthday to my fundraiser. This brought in another $600 and, more importantly, injected momentum back into my campaign.

People got excited, more people shared it, and there was a new air of optimism around the fundraiser. With an hour left in 2015, the last $50 was donated.

In January, we brought 900 nets into the village and held a huge training session with the villagers on how to install them. The local Malawian news station came to report on it. It felt so good to make a video of that completed project and send it back to donors.

The success of the "Village Fridays" series was a major signal that I was heading in the right direction. This was a thrilling time where I would wake up with pure excitement every day. I loved what I was doing, and it felt like the whole world around me was beginning to click into place. I was on the verge of finding the life calling I had so desperately wanted.

20

A LASTING TRANSFORMATION

A pattern had developed. Every time I asked for money, it always came in. Even when a campaign seemed to be dead in the water, something outside of my control happened to bring it back to life. I learned that when I pitched my vision to the world, the people who wanted to support me would find me and help make it happen.

I decided the next vision I pitched would be my largest yet.

At first, I thought about building a clinic in the village to address Malawi's high pregnancy mortality rate.

Blessings told me with confidence that this wasn't a good idea. There was no way to make it sustainable. We would have to raise money every year for upkeep and salaries. Plus, there was just no one to manage the whole operation.

Despite these objections, I insisted we move forward. There was too much momentum to give up.

To persuade me, Blessings came to my house, sat me down, and handed me a packet. He told me that the packet was put together by a woman named Tiya seven years ago. It was a full-blown plan for a girls' high school. It included the curriculum, the architecture plans, the location, and a path to sustainability.

The school was going to run on a 50/50 model. 50% of the girls would come from the city and pay higher tuition. The remaining 50% would be vulnerable girls from the village who showed lots of promise. The village girls would never be able to afford this level of education, but the addition of the city girls made the financials work. The economic diversity would serve to make both sets of girls more well-rounded.

This was a fantastic plan. The only thing needed was $100,000, which I would have to fundraise.

Before I fully committed, I sought out the most influential guy I knew in Malawi. He also happened to know Tiya. Without giving my plans away, I asked him, "Do you think Tiya would make a good headmistress if she were in charge of a school?"

Without hesitation, he replied, "I've been thinking about starting a school myself, and she would be the first person I'd hire."

I nodded and thought to myself, "This is it."

The story of how thousands of people came together to raise $100,000 to put a self-sustaining girls' school in rural Malawi is a whole book in and of itself. On September 5, 2016, 120 girls showed up to a fully staffed school building for the first day of classes. As a bonus, I knew that if and when these young women do get pregnant, they will have the necessary education to take care of themselves and their children.

For these girls, the cycle of poverty had been broken. This school changed the trajectory of their lives and the lives of their future children. I had the pleasure of witnessing this permanent, sustainable change that would have a powerful ripple effect.

I knew that helping to facilitate lasting transformations like this is what I was meant for. Now, I would just have to find a way to create these opportunities all over the world.

21

THE ONE-PAGE

In January of 2016, while I was working on plans for Girls Shine Academy, someone asked me the question, "What would be your dream job?" What came out of my mouth next surprised even me.

"I think I'd like to build a tech platform that's like an 'Uber' for charity."

That afternoon, I sat down at my desk and wrote a one-page description of what would eventually become DonorSee. DonorSee would use a network of vetted, on-the-ground aid workers to post projects. When the projects were funded, the aid workers would send video updates to the donors showing exactly how their money helped real people in need. So, if you donate hearing aids to a girl with deafness, you would get a video of her hearing for the first time.

Writing down the concept for DonorSee on that one-page was an odd experience. It came out of me, almost uncontrollably, in a burst of inspiration. I had finally found my life calling. Everything I had been working on up to this point all culminated in DonorSee.

For the first time, I began to see why I had met Emily, the girl in the purple dress. Emily was an orphan because Blessings didn't have the tools to communicate the importance of a $20 donation.

If DonorSee had existed at the time, Blessings would have been able to convey the genuine need for a trip to the hospital. He could have shown that Emily's mother was getting worse and worse, and would have had an easy way to raise the support needed to help her.

In life or death situations, DonorSee would allow donors to act immediately, as if walking across the street to help their neighbor.

While I was fundraising $100,000 to build Girls Shine Academy, I was also fundraising an additional $150,000 in the background to launch DonorSee.

I knew that after Girls Shine Academy was complete,

people would be eager to latch onto my next vision, no matter how big. On September 6th, the first day of classes, I sent the final video update to thank everyone who donated to the school. It was a list of several thousand people by this point. At the end of the video, I told them to check back in a few weeks for a big announcement. They had no idea I was getting ready to launch a new model for charity.

22

LAUNCH

On September 26, 2016, I released DonorSee to the world. The idea was instantly contagious, and donors poured in.

The concept was so popular that we kept running out of projects. It would take a while, but eventually, we trained enough aid workers to handle the growing volume of donations. Now we have a steady stream of vetted projects to which donors can give.

One of my favorite DonorSee stories involves a seven-year-old girl named Apulole from rural Africa. Apulole crossed a river to fetch water from a well for her family. While waist-deep in the river on her way home, she was attacked by a crocodile. Two men on shore jumped in, chased away the beast, and brought Apulole back onto dry land. She was bleeding badly. Thankfully, one of our on-the-ground partners was nearby who immediately posted Apulole's story to DonorSee, asking for $100. The project was funded within minutes, and Apulole was taken to a private hospital. Her life was saved, as her donors watched it all unfold in real time.

DonorSee has partnered with vetted aid workers in more than 50 countries to help people like Apulole who are going through a difficult life moment. Our donors get video updates every time they get involved. We have been featured in USA Today, NBC News, ABC News, HuffPost, and National Review, and I have had the opportunity to give many talks.

The amount of love and support for the vision of DonorSee has been an overwhelming gift and something I could have never predicted. People love that they can give directly to those with immediate needs as if they're lending a hand to their neighbor across the street.

23

NEIGHBOR, **REDEFINED**

When I moved from America to Malawi, I learned that the way I looked at the world was incomplete. I went from thinking I had below average material wealth to realizing I had spent all my life living in a pristine fish tank. While this realization was startling, it also gave my life a clear direction.

During the several years I lived in Malawi, I would often drive around and see people suffering right on the side of the road. Sometimes it was malnourished kids, and other times it was paraplegics begging for change. Seeing these people would remind me of the story of the Good Samaritan.

Jesus told a story about a traveler who had been beaten by robbers. He was left lying in agony on the side of the road. Two prominent community leaders were walking along the same street. They didn't stop to help the suffering traveler because they thought it was beneath them. A Samaritan, from a different town, then came along and halted his entire schedule to help the suffering traveler. The Samaritan not only found a place for the beaten man to recover but also paid for all his expenses. The Samaritan didn't physically live next door to the traveler, but, according to Jesus, he was the only one who acted like his neighbor that day.

My move from America to Malawi did more than illuminate my perspective on money. It also redefined who I saw as my neighbor.

I may currently live with my wife in Falls Church, VA so I can run DonorSee, but I know the people who qualify as my neighbors extend far beyond those who literally live next door. My neighbors include the people around the world who are ignored. The ones who are inconvenient to help.

I'm thankful that, because of where I was born, I've been put in a position to do something about global poverty. Without that life calling, I would still be aimlessly wandering around the halls of some corporate office. Instead, I wake up every day excited to work.

Learning to love the poor, as if they were next door, has given my life a rich purpose. I hope it will do the same for you.

PICTURES

2004 to 2019

Gret in Kenya | Gret petting a cheetah his first week in Kenya.

At Dulles | Gret and Woody at Dulles International Airport before boarding their first plane to Malawi.

Hiking Mulanje | Gret and roommates hiking Mt. Mulanje, third tallest mountain in Africa.

Hippo | The hippo that swam right under the capsized sailboat.

Math class | Gret with his Algebra 2 class.

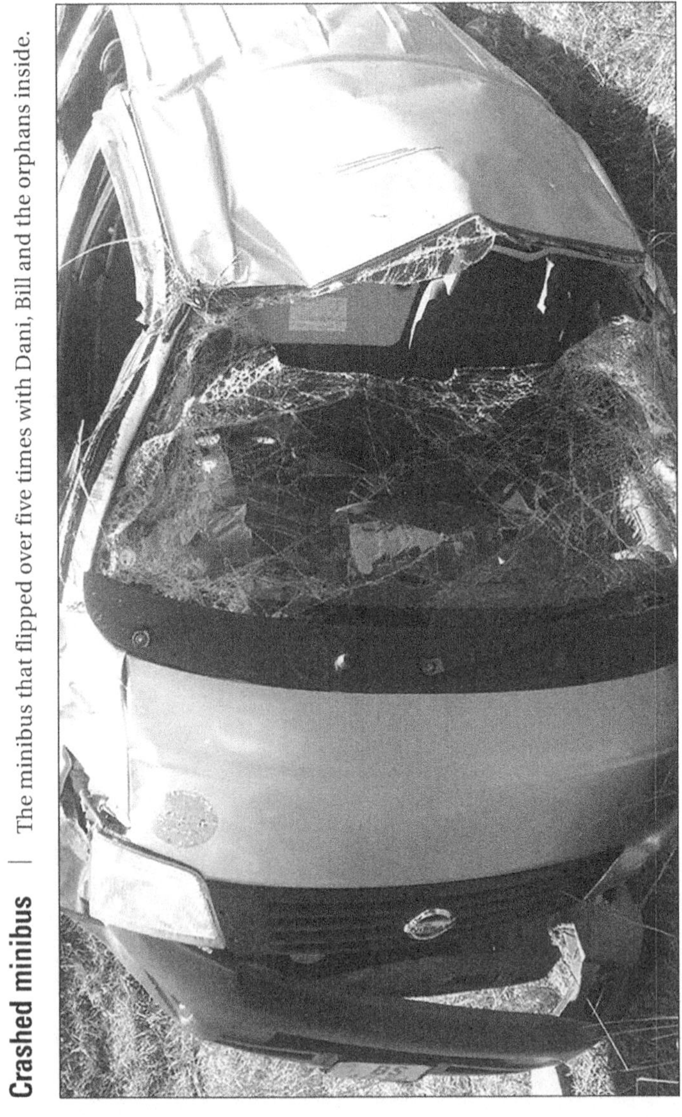

Crashed minibus | The minibus that flipped over five times with Dani, Bill and the orphans inside.

Marriage | Bill and Dani's wedding day.

Blessings | Blessings teaching kids during a Friday village trip.

Gret and Blessings | Blessings translating for Gret while he gives a talk in the village.

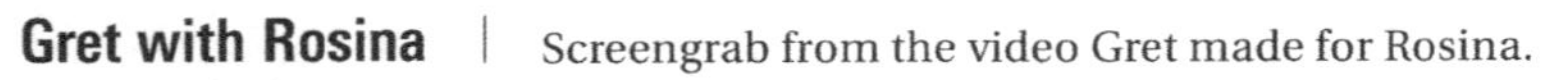

Gret with Rosina | Screengrab from the video Gret made for Rosina.

Rosina's old house | Where Rosina used to live.

Rosina's finished house | Where Rosina lives now. Picture taken during the rainy season.

Rosina greeting mom | Rosina shaking hands with my mom when she came to visit Malawi.

1.3 billion people live on less than **$1.25** a day

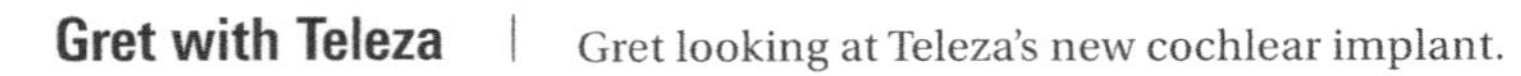

Gret with Teleza | Gret looking at Teleza's new cochlear implant.

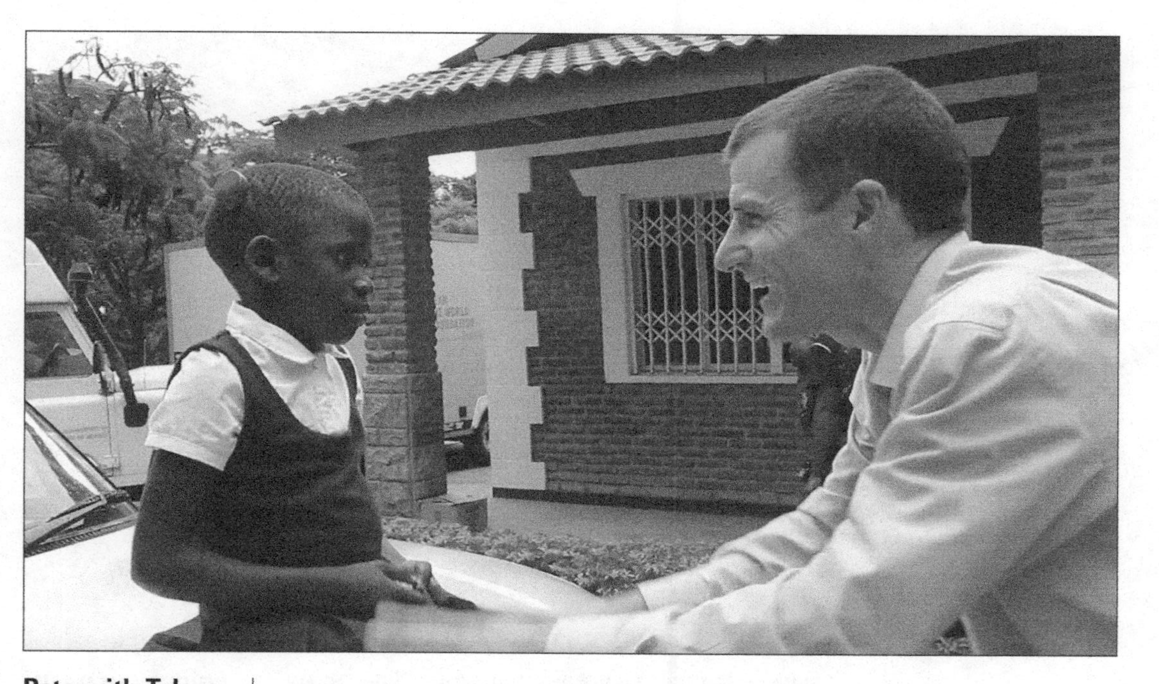

Pete with Teleza | Teleza with audiologist the first day she got her hearing back.

Mzati in hospital | Mzati being visited in the hospital by his best friend.

Mzati playing soccer | Mzati playing college soccer, present day in America.

Painting class | The painting class that raised money to build houses for widows.

BY NTCHINDI MEKI

Howm fighting malaria

HOUSING for Orphans and Widows in Malawi (Howm) Foundation, on Sunday donated over 900 mosquito nets worth K3.2 million to communities around Chibampha Village in Traditional Authority Malili in Lilongwe.

According to founder of the organisation, Gret Glyer, malaria remains a challenge in the area where he is also working in collaboration with another organisation called Live Love Malawi.

Speaking after presenting the donation, Glyer explained that during the time he has been to the area, a number of children under the age of five have died of malaria, hence the move to mobilize funds from well-wishers in the United States of America to assist the people.

"I did a research and established that out of 100 eople, 75 were testing ositive for malaria. I new there was something could do and that is to make available mosquito nets to the people because if 75 percent of people in this area are sleeping under mosquito nets, then malaria cases will drastically reduce," he said.

In her remarks, Village Head Malikha thanked the organisation for the donation, saying malaria cases have reached alarming levels in the area, especially following the onset of the rains.

She, however, expressed disappointment over the tendency by some people to sell nets.

Live Love Malawi Director, Blessings Chibambo, hailed the organisation for the gesture, saying the catchment area has a population of over 36,000 who need to be protected from diseases if they are to be productive citizens.

GLYER—There was something I could do

Malawi newspaper | Gret featured in Malawian newspaper about the mosquito net fundraiser.

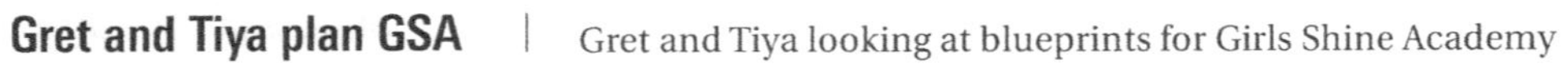

Gret and Tiya plan GSA | Gret and Tiya looking at blueprints for Girls Shine Academy

Drone shot of GSA | Drone shot of Girls Shine Academy with partially constructed classroom.

Emily | Emily's infectious smile from the passenger seat of Blessings' white truck.

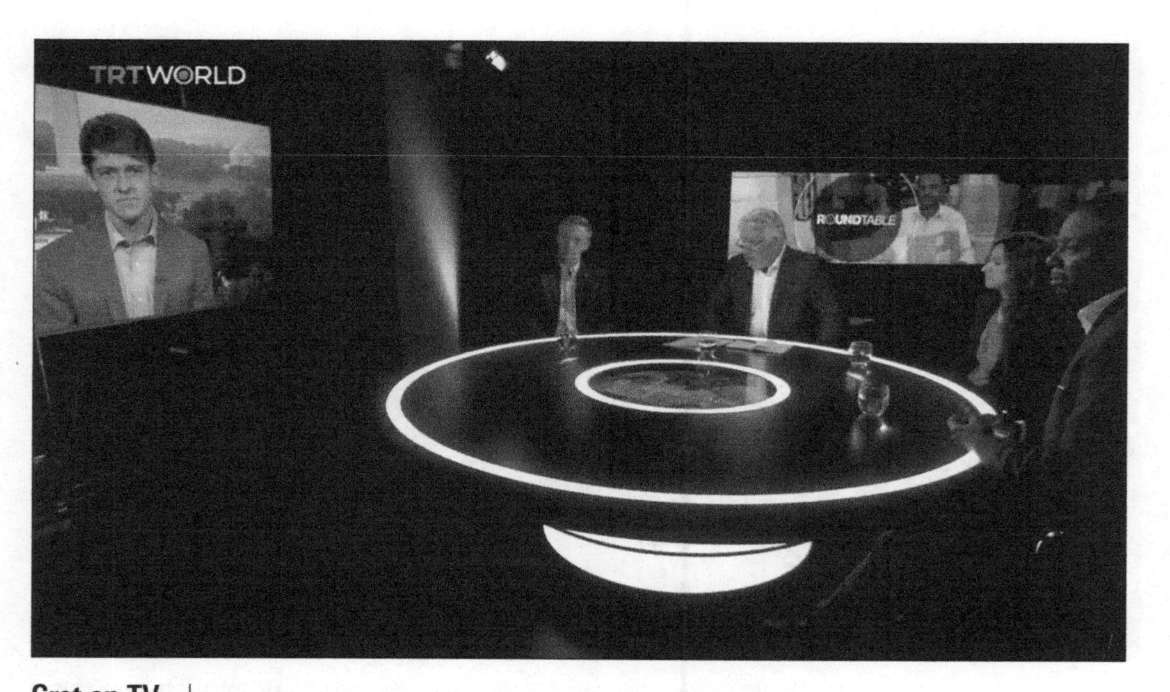

Gret on TV | Gret discussing DonorSee with panel on Round Table TV show.

Gret and Heather at GSA | Gret and his wife, Heather, visiting Girls Shine Academy in 2019.

Kickstarter thumbnail | Gret holding up manuscript for Kickstarter video for this book. Thank you again, supporters, for helping me tell my story.

2016 to present

EPILOGUE

When I first moved back to America to run DonorSee, I found myself annoyed at all the petty complaints I heard from people in the developed world. Whether it was slow internet, DC traffic, or subpar coffee, I had a tendency to stick my nose up at this level of entitlement.

I slowly learned to replace my anger with compassion. I would be just as entitled had I not spent three years living in the poorest country in the world. I had an experience that formed my perspective on money that most of my friends did not.

I've seen many people go overseas, come back, and then distinctly move on with their lives. Their mindset seems to be something like, "Well, I did my one year of service, so that's more than most people can say."

I see things differently. It's because of how deeply I know the issues others around the world face that I feel an even greater responsibility to do something about them.

I hope that, through my story, I've given you enough of a glimpse of these issues, that you feel a responsibility to do something about them, as well. It's easier now, more than ever before, to serve our widely ignored neighbors living in remote corners of the globe. This puts a high calling on all of us.

AFTERWORD

I never give people specific advice about money unless I'm asked. I don't tell people what percentage of their income they should donate and I don't make people feel bad about spending money on nice things. There are occasions for almost everything, and everyone faces a unique set of circumstances that factor into what they should do with their bank account.

I do have one piece of general advice with which I will leave you. When most people learn about global poverty, they find the issue so big and daunting, that they are prone to despair. It's okay to have this reaction for a time. I despaired when I thought I couldn't help Rosina. Eventually, you will want to move forward and do something. Especially once you realize that your involvement will make a life or death difference.

So, if you want to give a sufficient amount to those who need it, there's just one rule: *give until it hurts.* You will never feel satisfied with your own contribution until you have to experience some kind of sacrifice to make your giving possible.

I like to ask the question, "When was the last time you gave up a vacation so you could give more?" It's a question that makes people uncomfortable because we all love our vacations. It's these sorts of difficult questions that can encourage needed conversations about what our responsibility is to our neighbors around the world.

I hope this book sparks many uncomfortable conversations in your life and the lives of those around you.

GET INVOLVED

Anything I've ever done was only made possible because of the people who support me. If you believe in me and you believe in the work that I'm doing, I ask that you get involved in one of the three ways below.

Share This Book

More than you know, it makes a huge difference when you leave this book a review on Amazon. Please also consider buying extra copies to share.

Love Your Global Neighbors With DonorSee

DonorSee allows you to immediately get involved in the lives of real people in real need. You can either donate directly to them at *donorsee.com* or make a monthly commitment at *donorsee.com/monthly*.

Support Me

I don't take a salary for running DonorSee, despite it being a full-time job that takes up many nights and weekends. When you donate, you can rest assured that the CEO is getting absolutely 0% of your donation. Instead, I ask those who believe in me to support my work at *patreon.com/gretglyer*.

RESOURCES

Here are some resources that I would recommend if you are interested in learning more about poverty and charity.

1. **GretGlyer.com.** Visit my blog, subscribe to my YouTube channel, and listen to my podcast to stay up to date on my work.
2. **"The Boy Who Harnessed The Wind"** available on Netflix. This is a true story about a Malawian boy who learned to use a windmill to bring electricity to his local village. He also happened to attend the school I taught at for a year. This film will help you feel the everyday struggles of people living in extreme poverty.
3. **GlobalRichList.com.** This website will quickly show you just how wealthy you are. Everyone should check this out at least once in their lives.
4. **"When Helping Hurts"** by Steve Corbett and Brian Fikkert. My book doesn't spend much time talking about the potential pitfalls of trying to do good, but

there are plenty. *"When Helping Hurts"* will provide you with a healthy framework for how to tackle poverty alleviation.

5. **"Poverty, Inc."** available on Amazon Prime. In just 90 minutes you will get a quick summary of many of the concepts in which *"When Helping Hurts"* goes in depth.

I am not affiliated with any of these resources, but I do highly recommend them. If you ever need anything, you can always email me at gret@donorsee.com.

The global poverty facts you found scattered throughout this book were provided by UNICEF, World Health Organization, United Nations, Newsweek, International Nutrition Foundation, The Borgen Project, CNN, World Bank, and Our World In Data from reports completed between 2007 to 2019.

ABOUT THE AUTHOR

GRET GLYER

GRET GLYER is the CEO of DonorSee and has raised more than a million dollars for those in extreme poverty. From 2013 to 2016, Glyer lived with the world's poorest people in Malawi, Africa where he built more than 150 houses for the homeless, and crowdfunded $100,000 to build a girls' school in rural Malawi. Glyer has been featured in USA Today, National Review, HuffPo, Acton Institute, and is a TEDx Speaker.

Made in United States
Orlando, FL
01 August 2022